D1073344

Why Christians Should Study Apologetics

The Problem of Christian Anti-Intellectualism

Jefrey D. Breshears

Areopagus Publishing

Areopagus Publishing
www.TheAreopagus.org

"The Problem of Christian Anti-Intellectualism"
By Breshears, Jefrey D.

ISBN: 978-0-9830680-1-3

The Problem of Christian Anti-Intellectualism

"I must be frank with you: the greatest danger confronting American evangelical Christianity is the danger of anti-intellectualism." – Charles Malik

"The scandal of the evangelical mind is that there is not much of an evangelical mind." – Mark A. Noll

Several years ago I received a call from the minister of education in a church where I was teaching a course. He was interested to know how things were going, and I responded that everything appeared to be fine – there seemed to be quite a lot of interest, we were having spirited discussions, etc. After a minute or so he mentioned that the church staff had heard several comments about the class, but one person in particular had caught their attention when she remarked, "Dr. Breshears talks to us like we're intelligent!" The minister went on to say, "Now we [the staff] are all wondering what she meant by that. What's that supposed to say about us?" I just smiled and casually changed the subject. It seemed rather imprudent to point out any obvious implications.

If I had to choose between a clean heart or a sharp mind, I'd opt for the former without a doubt. After all, Jesus did say, "Blessed are the pure of heart" – not "Blessed are the mentally acute." But of course this is a false dilemma and a choice that we need not make. The example of Jesus himself provides ample evidence that one does not exclude the other. Nevertheless, many

Christians seem to think it's one or the other and that a fideistic (or purely intuitive) faith is somehow more "spiritual" than a belief system based on study and reflection. This orientation persists despite the clear warning of scripture that "It is not good to have zeal without knowledge" (Prov. 19:2).

No one should think the goal of the Christian life is to become a Christian intellectual (whatever that means). Many of the most sincere and devout Christians I know are not particularly cerebral by orientation. But it's one thing to be *un*intellectual by nature – there's no shame in that – but quite another thing to be *anti*intellectual by choice. *Anti*-intellectualism – intellectual laziness or an aversion to anything that requires mental effort – is not only unimpressive but contrary to what Jesus declared to be the greatest of all commandments: To love God with all our heart, soul, mind and strength. Does anyone seriously believe that we can honor God while living mindlessly, or practice wholistic discipleship without thinking deeply about our faith and relating it to every area of life?

Although America has always had more than its share of great thinkers, American culture in general is appallingly antiintellectual. Generally speaking, knowledge is not highly valued – or at least, knowledge of things that truly matter. (On the other hand, millions apparently have an insatiable curiosity when it comes to the private lives of celebrities.) In a culture that values entertainment over most everything else, Socrates' dictum that "The unexamined life is not worth living" has been replaced by the notion that "The unexciting life is not worth living." This has been the theme of some of the great works in social criticism over the past eighty years from Aldous Huxley's *Brave New World* to Neil Postman's *Amusing Ourselves To Death*, Christopher Lasch's *The Culture of Narcissism* and Jacques Barzun's *From Dawn To Decadence* – all of which should be required reading for anyone concerned about the decline of American culture.

Cultural Illiteracy

Over the past generation, due mostly to a misguided devotion to egalitarianism, America has become an LCD (Lowest Common Denominator) culture in which standards have plummeted in virtually every area of life. We see this not only in our educational, political and legal systems but also in the media, popular culture, and public and private morality. Regrettably, we also see it in the church where, under the guise of "relevancy," worship services are transformed into pop entertainment spectacles, homiletics (the art of preaching) degenerates into feel-good motivational rhetoric, and Christian education is reduced to fun-and-games activities for youth and mind-numbingly superficial "Bible study" for adults.

Twenty-five years ago E. D. Hirsch, a distinguished professor of English and humanities at the University of Virgiania, published a book that temporarily sent the American education establishment into convulsions. *Cultural Literacy: What Every American Needs to Know* (1986) exposed the utter bankruptcy of decades of educational experimentation that had rendered most Americans abysmally ignorant of the basic core knowledge on which our culture is founded. Hirsch cited surveys that indicated that most college students and adults

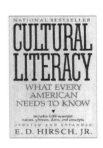

lack the basic knowledge to understand current events or otherwise function as informed and responsible citizens. He attributed the problem to John Dewey and other Progressive Education reformers who abandoned content-based learning in the early 20th century in favor of a skills-based approach that de-emphasized the accumulation of facts and knowledge, culminating in educational fads such as "values clarification" and (so-called) "critical thinking."* Predictably, the education establishment dismissed Hirsch's book as reactionary "academic fundamentalism" although Hirsch was in fact a mainstream liberal academician and definitely not a conservative.

[Note: More recently, comedian Jay Leno's "Jaywalking" segments, in which he interviews random people on the streets of Hollywood, confirm Hirsch's thesis, only in a considerably less scientific and more humorous vein. Some examples:

Leno: "Can you name two of the Founding Fathers?"
Interviewee: "Founding Fathers of what?"
Leno: "Can you name any of the Ten Commandments?"
Interviewee: "Uhhh... freedom of speech...."
Leno: "Who fiddled while Rome burned?"
Interviewee: "Who fiddled? Fiddled with what?"
Leno: "What was the Gettysburg Address?... Have you heard of it?"
Interviewee (dressed in a cap and gown at her college graduation ceremony): "Uh, yeah, I've heard of it, but I don't know the exact address."
Leno: "What is the opening line of the Bible?"
Interviewee: "Long ago in a galaxy far far away...."]

A year after Hirsch's book was released, University of Chicago educator Allan Bloom published *The Closing of the American Mind* (1987), in which he analyzed the philosophy behind the shift away from knowledge-based education.

* Regarding the emphasis on "values clarification" and "critical thinking," it should be noted that no systematic or standardized methodology has ever been established for assessing the success of such a curriculum. Certainly, there has been no effort to offer mandatory (or even elective) courses in either Natural Law theory or the principles of logic, without which "values clarification" and "critical thinking" degenerate into subjective and absurd free-for-alls. Few contemporary academicians accept the validity of traditional Natural Law, and logic is often disparaged as "Western thinking" (or in the opinion of radical feminist scholars, "male thinking").

According to Bloom, the major reason why modern education has been reduced to skill development and job training is because it is permeated with relativistic values. In his Introduction he noted that relativism is the cornerstone "virtue" on which all modern education is built:

> There is one thing a professor can be absolutely certain of: almost every student entering the university believes, or says he believes, that truth is relative....
>
> [Contemporary students] are unified only in their relativism and in their allegiance to equality.... The danger they have been taught to fear from absolutism is not error but intolerance. Relativism is necessary to openness, and this is the virtue, the only virtue, which all primary education for more than fifty years has dedicated itself to inculcating. [Allan Bloom, *The Closing of the American Mind* (1987), pp.25-26.]

In a similar vein, University of Texas philosophy professor J. Budziszewski recounts his first faculty job interview (prior to his conversion to Christianity) and how his confident commitment to relativism landed him the position:

> Twenty-four years ago I stood before the [political science] department at the University of Texas to give my 'here's-why-you-should-hire-me' lecture. Fresh out of grad school, I wanted to teach about ethics and politics, so I was showing the faculty my stuff. What did I tell them? First, that we human beings just make up our own definitions of what's good and what's evil; and second, that we aren't responsible for what we do, anyway. For that I was hired to teach. [J. Budziszewski, *How To Stay Christian in College* (2004), p. 18.]

To say the least, such a mentality poses a serious challenge to education because if everything is subjective, why bother subjecting students to the rigor of learning facts when, as Nietzsche declared, "truth" is no more than "a mobile army of metaphors." In other words, there is no truth and there are no facts – only opinions and interpretations. Or as the philosopher John Caputo of Syracuse University writes in *Radical Hermeneutics*, "The truth is that there is no truth."

Inspired by Hirsch's and Bloom's books and troubled by my own students' apparent lack of cultural literacy, I administered a 50-question exam to several hundred students at Georgia State University in the mid-1980s that covered a wide span of common names, terms, events, etc., including mind-benders such as...

- List the last four American presidents.
- What river forms the boundary between Texas and Mexico?
- What is the connotation of the term, "Wall Street" (i.e., what does it symbolize)?
- What issue was decided in the *Roe v. Wade* Supreme Court decision of 1973? and

- Who wrote the songs "Blowin' In the Wind," "The Times They Are A-changin'," and "Like a Rolling Stone?"

On a negative scale, the results exceeded my expectations. On a standard grading scale of 0 to 100, with 60 being the cut-off mark for a passing grade, over 90% of these students failed the test, and less than a fourth scored above the 50% mark. While nearly half could name the four former members of the Beatles, only about three in a hundred could list four current members of the U. S. Supreme Court. Almost two-thirds could identify Mikhail Gorbachev as the leader of the Soviet Union, but less than a third knew the names of Georgia's two senators. Only eight percent came reasonably close to approximating the population of the United States, with fully one-fourth estimating that it exceeds a billion. (One student was quite precise: 18.25 bazillion.) Even more troubling, 87% could not identify *Roe v. Wade* as the landmark court decision legalizing abortion.

In an article published in the *Atlanta Journal-Constitution*, I commented...

> Much has been written and discussed lately lamenting the apparent lack of knowledge regarding the fundamental core principles, institutions and traditions

upon which Western civilization in general and American culture in particular are based. In 1985 Congress required the National Endowment for the Humanities to prepare a status report on humanities education as part of the NEH's reauthorization legislation. In "American Memory: A Report on the Humanities in the Nation's Public Schools," the NEH concluded that the current history and literature curriculum offered in public schools is largely inadequate, that too much emphasis is placed on mastering skills to the detriment of subject content. Among its findings, "American Memory" revealed that over two-thirds of American high school graduates were unable to place the Civil War within the correct half-century.... [Jefrey D. Breshears, "Our Students' Minds Are a Cultural Disaster." *Atlanta Journal-Constitution* (Jan. 10, 1988), 6C.]

This situation would be alarming enough if it were limited only to "secular" issues, but of course this is not the case. More recently, and more to the point of Christian anti-intellectualism, Stephen Prothero, a religion professor at Boston University, has focused on the crisis state of religious illiteracy in his 2007 book, *Religious Literacy: What Every American Needs to Know – and Doesn't.*" In the Introduction Prothero relates a comment by a visiting professor from Austria that Americans are "very religious, but they know next to nothing about religion." Prothero observes that 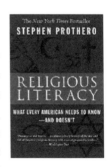 America, "one of the most religious countries on earth, is also a nation of religious illiterates," and confesses that early on in his academic career he unwittingly contributed to this knowledge deficit:

When I finished graduate school and became a professor myself, I told students that I didn't care about facts. I cared about having challenging conversations, and I offered my quiz-free classrooms as places to do just that. I soon found, however, that the challenging conversations I coveted were not possible without some common knowledge – common knowledge my students plainly lacked. And so, quite against my prior inclinations, I began testing them .... [Eventually] I became, like Hirsch, a traditionalist about content. [Stephen Prothero, *Religious Literacy: What Every American Needs to Know – and Doesn't* (2007), p. 4.]

In his book, Prothero points out that ignorance of Christianity and the Bible is not just a problem for non-Christians and secularists, and that self-described "born-again Christians" score only slightly better than other Americans on religious literacy surveys. Other studies, such as a highly publicized survey in 2010 by the Pew Forum on Religion & Public Life, support Prothero's bleak assessment. Even more disturbing, extensive research by the Barna Group over the past 25 years indicates that less than 10% of Americans hold a consistent biblical worldview, including the majority of professing Christians.

There is, of course, an inextricable connection between cultural literacy in general and religious knowledge in particular that Christians should especially value. Neither the Bible nor Christian history and theology can be understood outside their broader historical context – just as everything that happens in Christianity today is influenced by the events of our time and the culture in which we live. This means that those with little or no historical or cultural consciousness will always have at best a superficial understanding of Scripture, Christian history and the present state of the church. Nothing that happens in history, including the life and ministry of Jesus, occurs in an historical vacuum, and it is impossible to adequately understand either the narrative or the meaning of Christ's life without some degree of historical and cultural literacy. This awareness alone should prompt Christians to value and pursue knowledge if for no other reason than to understand the Bible, the Christian faith and tradition, and the role of the church in contemporary society.

The Causes

So who (or what) is responsible for the current deficit in religious and cultural knowledge in our society, particularly among Christians? There are four factors to be considered:

(1)One obvious source is the failure of parents to impart at least a rudimentary level of religious literacy to their children. The home should provide a rich pedagogical environment for the transmission of true knowledge, manners and morals, but regrettably many parents fail to maximize the opportunities that these precious years afford. When a child can grow up and live in a home for at least 18 years (that's more than 157,000 hours) without ever learning anything substantive about the Bible and the Christian faith (or other religions, for that matter), the fundamental responsibility for the failure undoubtedly rests on the parents.

(2)For its part, public education (and much of private education) contributes significantly to the problem by excluding religion from the academic curriculum under the misguided notion that it otherwise would violate the principle of separation of church and state. Not only is religionless education seriously deficient, but it actually promotes a secularistic worldview that is innately anti-religious.

(3)Popular culture – particularly, TV, movies and music – is a pervasive influence in American life, yet it rarely presents anything but a critical or satirical view of Christianity. The anti-Christian bias in contemporary popular culture is stunning, to say the least, but in fact this has been the case throughout most of the 20th century. Even in the conventional 1950s, TV, movies and music rarely acknowledged religious issues or even hinted that the Christian faith is a significant factor in American life. (How often was God ever mentioned in *Leave It To Beaver* or *Father Knows Best*, or how many times were Ricky Ricardo and Lucy or Ozzie and Harriet ever shown in church?) While not as explicitly hostile to Christian values as contemporary pop culture, nonetheless television shows, movies and music in the '50s marginalized Christianity to the point of irrelevancy.

(4)The fourth factor, and in many respects the most troubling, is the current state of church-based Christian education. Several of the questions on my "Cultural Literacy Quiz" were religious-based or had religious connotations, including...

- What is the name of the current pope, and what nationality is he? (Note: Much had been made of the fact that Pope John Paul II was Polish and the first non-Italian pope in several centuries.)
- What is the largest Christian denomination in the U.S.?
- What issue was decided in the *Roe v. Wade* Supreme Court decision of 1973?
- Who wrote most of the books of the New Testament? (Less than 20% answered "the apostle Paul" or "St. Paul," and other responses ranged from Moses, John the Baptist and Jesus to "King James" and "Nobody knows.")

Considering my students' lack of religious literacy in general and Bible knowledge in particular, I occasionally ruminated on the implications. Assuming that children can begin learning Bible stories and retaining basic Bible knowledge at about age four, and supposing that about half of my students grew up attending church at least half of the time, they would have logged nearly 400 hours in church (or 800 hours if they attended both church and Sunday School) by the time they entered college. Now if students were exposed to arithmetic or English grammar or U.S. history for several hundred hours, we might reasonably expect them to know something about the subject by the time they got to college. Yet very few of my students seemed to know much of anything when it came to the Bible and Christianity. (Of course, most didn't seem to know much about history, either.)

The troubling fact is that Christian parents aren't the only ones to blame for their children's ignorance of the Christian faith. Churches also share much of the responsibility. When such things are not discussed informally and as a matter of course at home and around the dinner table, the message to children is that "religion" is merely a Sunday obligation rather than a lifestyle and a comprehensive worldview. Then, when children and youth are not challenged at church to think deeply about their faith and relate it to the broader issues of life, it becomes merely a tedious ritual with little relation to the "real" world.

Most evangelical churches, at least to some extent, emphasize theology – i.e., *what* we are supposed to believe about God and morality – but very few emphasize apologetics – i.e., *why* we should believe these things. In the vast majority of churches, neither adults nor young people are challenged to explore in any real depth the factual and rational bases for the Christian faith.

For most Christians, theirs is essentially a subjective, emotion-driven and/or merely inherited faith devoid of any intellectual substance. Relatively few demonstrate anything other than a superficial understanding of the Bible, and even fewer are well-versed in Christian theology, church history and apologetics. The result, inevitably, is that most cannot adequately defend what they purport to believe – even when trying to share their faith with their children. This explains why, as Barna's research reveals, more than three-quarters of young adult Christians lose their faith when they go off to college. It also explains, at least in part, the reluctance of most Christian adults to stand up for their beliefs publicly or at work.

I'm always dismayed when I hear pastors or other Christians repeat the fideistic mantra that "We just have to believe" some theological or moral proposition with no explanation as to *why* such a belief is warranted. If there is one problem that the church doesn't have today, it is that too many Christians think too much. On the contrary, a major reason why Christianity has been on the defensive for 150 years is that Christians haven't been thinking enough. For the most part, we have forfeited the great intellectual battles of the last century-and-a-half to secularists and other anti-Christian skeptics, and then we wonder why we are losing the culture war. As mentioned earlier, the fact is that much of the church today is not merely *un*intellectual but defiantly *anti-*

intellectual. As the Christian philosopher William Lane Craig has written:

> Churches are filled with Christians who are idling in intellectual neutral. As Christians, their minds are going to waste. One result of this is an immature, superficial faith....
>
> The church is perishing today through a lack of thinking, not an excess of it. [William Lane Craig, *Reasonable Faith* (1984, 1994), pp. xiv, xv.]

The Consequences

We are often reminded that we live in a post-Christian culture, but many Christians fail to understand that we are losing the culture war (at least in part) because we have essentially forfeited the intellectual war. Ideas have consequences, and history has shown that what is intellectually respectable becomes, over time, socially acceptable and culturally normative.

In the late 19th and early 20th centuries, a few Christian leaders understood that the church, in order to uphold the credibility of the gospel, must stand up to the challenges posed by theological liberalism, scientism, Darwinism, Marxism, Freudianism and other challenges to the faith. In an article in the *Princeton Theological Review* in 1913 entitled "Christianity and Culture," John Gresham Machen, a renowned Princeton theologian, warned that if Christians failed to adequately address the great intellectual challenges of the day, the gospel would be put on the defensive and evangelism would be seriously hampered. Machen wrote that "False ideas are the greatest obstacles to the reception of the gospel," and that passionate evangelism would experience only sporadic success "if we permit the whole collective thought of the nation" [i.e., the *Zeitgeist* – the "spirit of the times"] to fall under the influence of anti-Christian philosophies. In such a culture Christianity would become privatized, excluded from the public square, and generally dismissed as little more than "a harmless delusion." The solution, according to Machen, was for Christians to become actively engaged in the great intellectual controversies of the day and take the battle to the enemy on their own ground in the universities and seminaries.

Unfortunately, Machen's warning went largely unheeded. Christians generally failed to respond to the intellectual challenges of the 20th century, and today we are reaping the consequences. As a result, a general lack of intellectual preparation has left many Christians confused, vulnerable and timid when it comes to defending truth. As Dinesh D'Souza observes in *What's So Great About Christianity*, "Instead of engaging [the] secular world, most Christians have taken the easy way out" and "retreated into a Christian subculture." But it is a weak subculture that lacks the necessary intellectual and countercultural self-awareness to withstand the constant pressures and unrelenting temptations of mainstream culture.

In a *Christianity Today* article in 1980 entitled "The Other Side of Evangelism," Charles Malik, a former Lebanese ambassador to the U.S., labeled anti-intellectualism the greatest weakness in evangelical Christianity because it undermines the credibility of our testimony. With great eloquence, Malik challenged Christians – particularly Christian young people – to take their education seriously and, regardless of their chosen vocation, prepare for a lifetime of effective ministry.

I must be frank with you: the greatest danger confronting American evangelical Christianity is the danger of anti-intellectualism. The mind in its greatest and deepest reaches is not cared for enough. But intellectual nurture cannot take place apart from profound immersion for a period of years in the history of thought and the spirit....

It will take a different spirit altogether to overcome this great danger of anti-intellectualism....

For the sake of greater effectiveness in witnessing to Jesus Christ himself, as well as for their own sakes, evangelicals cannot afford to keep on living on the

periphery of responsible intellectual existence. [Charles
Malik, "The Other Side of Evangelism." *Christianity Today*
(Nov. 7, 1980), p. 40.]

The problem of Christian anti-intellectualism has been a
recurring theme among evangelical thinkers in recent decades. In
1994 the church historian Mark Noll of Wheaton College wrote
The Scandal of the Evangelical Mind, alternately a survey of the rich
intellectual tradition that animated evangelical Christianity in the
17th and 18th centuries and a scathing critique of the precipitous
decline in the intellectual culture of mainstream evangelicalism
since the mid-19th century. So impressed were the editors of
Christianity Today magazine that they awarded *The Scandal of the
Evanglical Mind* their Book of the Year for 1994, but in general it
did little to awaken an intellectually flaccid and lethargic church
that has generally lost the ability to think. Noll was unsparing in
his denunciation of pop evangelicalism as he wrote...

The scandal of the evangelical mind is that there is
not much of an evangelical mind.... Notwithstanding all
their other virtues, American evangelicals are not
exemplary for their thinking, and they have not been so
for several generations.

Despite dynamic success at a popular level,
American evangelicals have failed notably in sustaining
serious intellectual life. They have nourished millions of
believers in the simple verities of the gospel but have
largely abandoned the universities, the arts, and other
realms of "high" culture.... Evangelicals sponsor dozens
of theological seminaries, scores of colleges, hundreds
of radio stations, and thousands of unbelievably diverse
parachurch agencies – but not a single research
university or a single periodical devoted to in-depth
interaction with modern culture....

By "the mind" or "the life of the mind," I am not
thinking primarily of theology as such...

By an evangelical "life of the mind" I mean more the
effort to think like a Christian – to think within a
specifically Christian framework – across the whole
spectrum of modern learning, including economics and

political science, literary criticism and imaginative writing, historical inquiry and philosophical studies, linguistics and the history of science, social theory and the arts.... Failure to exercise the mind for Christ in these areas has become acute in the twentieth century. That failure is the scandal of the evangelical mind. [Mark A. Noll, *The Scandal of the Evangelical Mind* (1994), pp. 3*ff.*]

In his book, *Love Your God with All Your Mind*, philosopher J. P. Moreland asks the reader to imagine a church filled with people who are intellectually shallow, self-absorbed and easily manipulated by the latest pop culture fads. As Moreland describes it, such a church would lack the theological depth, the strength of character and the necessary faith to stand against the grinding pressures and seductive temptations of contemporary life. He asks, "What would be the theological understanding, the evangelistic courage, [and] the cultural penetration of such a church?" The following points summarize his conclusions:

- It all comes down to priorities. If the cultivation of one's interior life is not a priority, there is inadequate motivation to invest the necessary time and effort developing an intellectually- and spiritually-mature life.

- Those who are intellectually lazy lack the motivation and the discipline to read and study, preferring instead to be entertained.

- If one is overly sensate in orientation, music and visual media will be more appealing than words on a page or abstract thoughts that require mental effort to process.

- If one is over-stimulated, cannot focus and is constantly hurried and distracted, he/she will have little patience for theoretical knowledge and too short an attention span to stay with an idea that is being carefully developed.

- If they read at all, self-absorbed people who are emotionally and intellectually immature will most likely gravitate toward books about Christian celebrities, the latest Christian pop fiction, or self-help books filled with simplistic moralizing and a superficial treatment of complex issues that place no demands on the reader.

- Christians who are emotionally and intellectually immature avoid substantive books that challenged readers to think deeply about the Christian faith or call them to a deeper level of commitment.

- Such a church filled with such people would be impotent in terms of standing against the powerful forces of narcissism, secularism, materialism and hedonism that dominate our contemporary culture.

- Furthermore, such a church, thoroughly coopted by the value system of modern American culture, would offer no countercultural or prophetic message.

- Such a church would measure her success primarily in terms of numbers – numbers that would be achieved primarily by watering-down and dumbing-down the gospel message and by catering to shallow and self-absorbed Christians.

- Eventually, such a church would become "her own grave digger," and her means of short-term success would turn out to be the very thing that would render her irrelevant in the long run. [J. P. Moreland, *Love Your God with All Your Mind* (1997), pp. 93-94.]

Of course, what makes Moreland's hypothetical scenario so troubling is that it's not hypothetical at all. Unfortunately, we don't really have to imagine such a church filled with such people because, in reality, this generally characterizes most churches and, frankly, too many church leaders. With such a mentality so prevalent in contemporary Christianity, is it any wonder why Christians are having so little impact on our society and culture? Is it any mystery why we are losing the culture war and why, with each passing decade, our society is growing increasingly rude, crude and lewd? We are not losing the culture war because the Christian belief system lacks truth and integrity. Essentially, we are losing the culture war by default. Having been co-opted by the values of our culture – not the least of which is a narcissistic, undisciplined and anti-intellectual approach to life – we have little to offer in terms of any convincing countercultural witness. As with all religions, people identify with Christianity for a variety of reasons. Many find great psychological comfort in their faith as a source of peace, joy and fulfillment in this life, along with the belief that a loving and benevolent God will preserve their souls for all of eternity. Others take a purely pragmatic approach and hope that if there is an afterlife, their religious faith will save them from eternal hellfire and damnation. For others, it's mostly about the satisfaction they attain from the social relationships they develop in church. And of course there are always those who are motivated primarily by economic and business considerations, or even by the political advantages that church membership can offer.

But ultimately, there is really only one reason why anyone should want to be a Christian: because it is *true*. The fundamental issue is not how our faith makes us feel or the benefits it offers, but does it correspond to reality? The Christian faith makes certain exclusive truth claims that, if false, render the Christian faith fraudulent and unimportant. However, if these truth claims are true, they elevate the Christian faith to the level of infinite importance. And in order to be true, the Christian faith must be intellectually coherent, consistent and credible. In other words, it must be factual and rational. It cannot be based on subjective feelings, intuition and personal experience alone.

This is always a difficult concept to convey because people naturally want to identify with a religion in order to derive certain benefits from it. In his essay on Christian apologetics, C.S. Lewis addressed this perennial problem with characteristic bluntness:

> One of the great difficulties [in sharing the gospel] is to keep before the audience's mind the question of Truth. They always think you are recommending Christianity not because it is *true* but because it is good. And in the discussion they will constantly try to escape

into stuff about the Spanish Inquisition [or the Crusades]... or anything whatever. You have to keep forcing them back... to the real point. Only thus will you be able to undermine ... their belief that a certain amount of 'religion' is desirable but one mustn't carry it too far. One must keep on pointing out that Christianity is a statement which, if false, is of no importance, and if true, of infinite importance. The only thing it cannot be is moderately important....

The great difficulty is to get modern audiences to realize that you are preaching Christianity solely because you think it is true; they always suppose you are preaching it because you like it or think it is good for society or something of that sort.... This immediately helps them to realize that what is being discussed is a question about objective fact – not about ideals and points view.... Do not water down Christianity. ["Christian Apologetics," in *Undeception: Essays on Theology and Ethics*.]

I am often puzzled by how entrenched fideism is in our churches and how much resistance there is to apologetics. We are often reminded, "You can't argue someone into the Kingdom of God." True enough, but we also can't *love* someone into the Kingdom, either. In fact, we cannot maneuver or manipulate anyone into responding sincerely and affirmatively to the grace of God. No one comes to faith unless the power of the Holy Spirit is at work in his heart, drawing him to Christ. But what apologetics can certainly do is to break down barriers to faith by exposing and dissolving erroneous arguments and irrational prejudices against belief in Christ, and by defending the historical and philosophical integrity of the Christian faith and worldview. And that in itself makes apologetics infinitely valuable. As is sometimes said of art, "Apologetics needs no justification."

One might think that for many Christians, a belief system based on evidence and reason is somehow less spiritual than a factless and irrational leap of faith. As William Lane Craig notes in his book, *Passionate Conviction*, "Sometimes people try to justify their lack of intellectual engagement by asserting that they prefer having a 'simple faith.' But here I think we must distinguish between a childlike faith and a childish faith." This is a vital distinction. A childlike faith is one that recognizes our total dependence upon our Heavenly Father. A childish faith, on the other hand, is immature, self-centered, unreflective and purely emotion-driven. It is all the difference between being "simple" rather than "simplistic" (or simple-minded). I have always appreciated the theme of the old hymn, "Tis a gift to be simple," but I would add, "Tis a shame to be a simpleton." Being created in the *imago Dei* – the image of God – we have been endowed with a mind capable of both creative and rational thought, and we should endeavor to honor God with all of our mental faculties.

Anti-intellectualism detracts from the credibility of our message and the attractability of our faith. On a personal level, people may like or even admire us, but rightly or wrongly they will take us and our beliefs far more seriously if they can respect us intellectually.

The Calling
We live in a Lowest Common Denominator culture in which low standards and mediocrity are acceptable norms in many areas of life. Unfortunately, this is as much of a problem in many Christian families and churches as it is in our culture in general. But scripture is clear that as followers of Jesus Christ we are called to a higher standard, and part of that high calling is to honor and serve God not only with our passion and our will, but also with our mind.

As Christians we are called to be apologists – defenders of the faith – just as we're all called to be evangelists (or witnesses) for

Christ. In fact, in our multi-cultural and pluralistic society today, evangelism without apologetics is mostly an exercise in futility. In I Peter 3:15 believers are exhorted to "sanctify (or "set apart") Christ as Lord in your heart," to "always be prepared to give an answer to everyone who asks you to give the reason for the hope that you have," and to "do this with gentleness and respect." Like the Great Commission, the call to be an apologist is not optional. This requires that we study and reflect upon what we believe so as to broaden and deepen our faith, and this is a process that takes intentionality, commitment and mental effort. But those who take this calling seriously find that it becomes a labor of love and that the rewards, both for ourselves as well as for others, often exceed our imagination.

The goal of the Christian life is not to be an intellectual but to be like Jesus. Spiritual maturity, not intellectual brilliance, is what ultimately matters. But in Jesus we find a man who was motivated not only by love and compassion but also by truth. In Jesus we find not only the world's greatest mystic and spiritual guru but the world's greatest philosopher and theologian. As our ideal, we find in him someone in perfect spiritual harmony with God the Father, and as our model, we find in him the perfect integration of passion, intellect and will.

By vocation I am an historian and an apologist, but by nature I am a contemplative Christian, and it is the cultivation of my soul and my communion with God through the internal presence of the Holy Spirit that I value the most. Nonetheless, I find that there is a symbiotic relationship between spiritual formation and an active mind, and I am convinced that the two are inseparable. If we truly desire to become more Christlike, we will progressively take on "the mind of Christ" as we deepen our communion with him. The apostle Paul clearly understood this connection as he declared in his exhortation to the Christians in Rome:

> Therefore, I urge you... in view of God's mercy, to
> offer your bodies as living sacrifices, holy and pleasing
> to God. This is your spiritual act of worship. Do not

conform any longer to the thought-patterns and lifestyles of this world, but be transformed by the renewing of your mind. Then you will be able to test and approve God's good and perfect will. [Rom. 12:1-2]

The Solution

In this essay I have sought to draw attention to the problem of Christian anti-intellectualism, the sources of the problem, the consequences, and our calling as followers of Jesus Christ to transcend the mediocrity of contemporary status quo Christianity. It is beyond the scope of this essay to offer detailed solutions to the problem.

But fortunately solutions do exist, and many excellent programs and resources are available for those who desire to broaden and deepen their commitment to Christ and their understanding of the Christian faith. For children, there are two programs that are particularly outstanding: the Montessori-based Catechesis of the Good Shepherd (www.cctheo.org) and the Bible-based AWANA program (www.awana.org).

For college students and adults there is a wealth of apologetical literature and resources – of which perhaps 80% or more has been produced in just the past 15-20 years. At the Areopagus we offer a systematic seminary-level curriculum that includes a 7-semester sequence of courses in apologetics and a 6-semester series in Christian history in addition to numerous other seminars in contemporary cultural studies and other topics. (See page 27 for a recommended reading list in Christian apologetics.)

Yet despite all the impressive resources that are available in apologetics, philosophy and cultural studies, the average church-going Christian is hardly aware that this material exists. If one were to ask why this is the case, the answer is obvious: the blockage comes at the pastoral level. Most Christians get not only much of their information about the Christian life but also their general orientation from their pastor. But unfortunately, relatively few pastors, youth ministers and even ministers of education have studied philosophy or apologetics at the university or seminary level, so most are largely oblivious to all the cutting-edge research and writing that has been going on in these fields in recent decades.

Too often, pastors and other ministers still regard philosophy and apologetics as tangential to the "real" goal of the gospel, which is saving souls. They fail to understand that in our pluralistic society, apologetics and effective evangelism are inextricably connected. The time is long-gone when a Christian might prevail in a disagreement with a nonbeliever by simply citing Scripture as his authority because, regrettably, there is less respect for the Bible today in mainstream society than ever before. For us to make a compelling case for Christ, it is imperative that we acquire the necessary knowledge and tactics that, to paraphrase the apostle Paul, "demolish spiritual strongholds, erroneous arguments, and every pretension that sets itself up against the knowledge of God in order to take captive every thought to make it obedient to Christ" [2 Cor. 10:4-5]. In this respect, apologetics is indispensable.

Christians who are not content with mediocrity in their own life should not settle for it in their church. Most ministers and church staff are committed Christians who are sincerely dedicated to serving others. The tendency, however, is to think "inside the box" and merely follow the latest trends or the path of least resistance. In a spirit of love and service, Christian parents should insist that their church provide the highest quality Christian education possible for their children and become actively involved in it. We have only one opportunity to raise our children, and anything other than the best should be unacceptable.

Likewise, the quality of adult education in most of our churches needs to be seriously upgraded, which might require some radical changes in Sunday School and the Wednesday night schedule. Rather than the traditional Sunday School system of dividing members up into permanent self-contained classes based on age (and even sex), churches could offer creative and stimulating semester-length courses on a variety of topics related to Biblical studies, theology, church history, apologetics, comparative worldviews and religions, contemporary cultural issues, science and the Christian faith, Christianity in literature and the arts, and even philosophy.

If churches lack qualified teachers for such specialized courses, there are two options:

(1)Organize discussion groups around video lectures and seminars.

(2)Recruit gifted teachers in various subject fields from local universities, seminaries or other churches. If churches in a community began sharing their resources, including their human resources, it would be mutually beneficial to all. As a Christian education and resource ministry in the metro-Atlanta area, the Areopagus specializes in this kind of adult education, and in most cities there are gifted Christians who are knowledgeable in at least some of these fields of study who would be eager to share their expertise within a network of associated churches.

What would be intolerable, not to mention totally unnecessary, would be to continue on as we have in the past. There is no reason to settle for mediocrity, and for the sake of the gospel the time has come to deal decisively with the problem of Christian anti-intellectualism. Of all people, Christians should be the most thoughtful, the most inquisitive, and the most creative as we strive to fulfill our calling to love and honor God with all our heart, with all our soul, and with all our mind.

And that is why Christians should study apologetics.

■

Jefrey Breshears, Ph.D., is a Christian historian, apologist, and the founder and president of The Areopagus, a Christian education ministry and study center in the Atlanta area that offers seminars and forums in Christian history, apologetics, Christian spirituality, and contemporary cultural issues.

JBreshears@TheAreopagus.org

Questions for Reflection and Discussion

1. What is the thesis (main point) of this essay?
2. Which point in this essay affected you the most, and why?
3. In what areas of American life have standards declined in recent decades?
4. Why is it so imperative that Christians be culturally-literate?
5. Which of the four causes of religious and cultural illiteracy have been most problematic in your life, and why?
6. What is the connection between theology (i.e., Christian doctrines and teachings) and apologetics?
7. How do your relate and respond to the quote by William Lane Craig on page 12?
8. What is your reaction to the quotes by Charles Malik and Mark Noll on pages 13-15?
9. Assess your own church in light of the points J. P. Moreland makes on pages 15-16.
10. What is the main point of the C. S. Lewis quote on page 17-18?
11. Why is Christian apologetics essential to effective evangelism?
12. Does your church make substantive Christian education a priority? What other priorities take precedence over education in your church? Where should quality Christian education rank on the priority scale, and why?

Notes and Reflections

....
....
....
....
....
....
....
....
....
....
....
....
....
....
....
....
....
....
....
....
....

20 Recommended Books
In Christian Apologetics

There is a wealth of excellent apologetics literature and resources available, the vast majority of which have been produced in the past 15-20 years. The following is not a ranked list, but simply progresses from more general works in apologetics (textbooks, handbooks, etc.) to more specific topics (e.g., the historicity of Jesus Christ, the Resurrection, science and the Christian faith, etc.). All are highly recommended.

1. **C. S. Lewis,** *Mere Christianity* (HarperSanFrancisco, 1952).

2. **Norman L. Geisler,** *Baker Encyclopedia of Christian Apologetics* (BakerBooks, 1999).

3. **J. P. Moreland and William Lane Craig,** *Philosophical Foundations for a Christian Worldview* (InterVarsity Press, 2003).

4. **Douglas Groothuis,** *Christian Apologetics: A Comprehensive Case for Biblical Faith* (IVP Academic, 2011).

5. **Josh McDowell,** *The New Evidence That Demands a Verdict* (Thomas Nelson Publishers, 1999).

6. **James W. Sire,** *The Universe Next Door: A Basic Worldview Catalog* (1976, 2004).

7. **Gregory Koukl,** *Tactics: A Game Plan for Discussing Your Christian Convictions* (Zondervan, 2009).

8. **Lee Strobel,** *The Case for Christ* (Zondervan, 1998).

9. **Lee Strobel,** *The Case for Faith* (Zondervan Publishing House, 2000).

10. **Lee Strobel,** *The Case for a Creator* (Zondervan, 2004).

11. **Norman L. Geisler and Frank Turek,** *I Don't Have Enough Faith To Be an Atheist* (Crossway Books, 2004).

12. Antony Flew, *There Is a God: How the World's Most Notorious Atheist Changed His Mind* (HarperOne, 2007).

13. J. Ed Komoszewski, M. James Sawyer and Daniel B. Wallace, *Reinventing Jesus: How Contemporary Skeptics Miss the Real Jesus and Mislead Popular Culture* (Kregel Publications, 2006).

14. Gary R. Habermas and Michael R. Licona, *The Case for the Resurrection of Jesus* (Kregel Publications, 2004).

15. Dinesh D'Souza, *What's So Great About Christianity* (Regnery Publishing, Inc., 2007).

16. J. P. Moreland, *Kingdom Triangle: Recover the Christian Mind, Renovate the Soul, Restore the Spirit's Power* (Zondervan, 2007).

17. Nancy R. Pearcey, *Total Truth: Liberating Christianity From Its Cultural Captivity* (Crossway Books, 2004).

18. Nancy R. Pearcey and Charles B. Thaxton, *The Soul of Science: Christian Faith and Natural Philosophy* (Crossway Books, 1994).

19. Stanley N. Gundry, J. P. Moreland and John Mark Reynolds, eds., *Three Views on Creation and Evolution* (Zondervan, 1999).

20. Jay Richards, ed., *God and Evolution* (Discovery Institute Press, 2010).

Notes and Reflections

....

....

....

....

....

....

....

....

....

....

....

....

....

....

....

....

....

....

....

....

....

....

....

Notes and Reflections

....

....

....

....

....

....

....

....

....

....

....

....

....

....

....

....

....

....

....

....

....

....

....

....

24916840R00020

Made in the USA
Lexington, KY
10 August 2013